day of the dachshund

ALSO BY JIM DRATFIELD

The Love of a Lab

Pug Shots

A Dog for All Seasons

Quotable Canines

Dogography

Dogphoria

Catography

Pug Nation

The Quotable Equine

The Quotable Feline

The Quotable Canine

Underdogs

day of the dachshund

jim dratfield

LYONS
PRESS

Guilford, Connecticut

An imprint of Globe Pequot

Distributed by NATIONAL BOOK NETWORK

British Library Cataloguing in Publication Information Available
Library of Congress Cataloging-in-Publication Data Available

ISBN 978-1-4930-2755-2 (hardcover)
ISBN 978-1-4930-2756-9 (e-book)

♾™ The paper used in this publication meets the minimum requirements of American National Standard for Information Sciences—Permanence of Paper for Printed Library Materials, ANSI/NISO Z39.48-1992.

To my dear son Phineas, while I know
that this isn't your first dedication I just
can't help myself but to do it all again!
I love you that much.

introduction

THE THING YOU NOTICE RIGHT OFF THE BAT IS a dachshund's absurdly comical shape. Designed like no other dog, they take themselves very, very seriously despite the humorous implications that their squatty and prolonged physiques have to offer. They bay and they bark like a dog ten times their size. Never intimidated by larger breeds, dachshunds will hold their own, thank you very much. A dachshund will captivate you with their waggish waddle and enthrall you with their roguish charm. The dachshund owner is smitten by these lovable louts. Dachshunds: so much fun to engage with, so much fun to photograph. I so enjoyed putting quip to canine in this book and I hope that you will guffaw, chortle, and smile broadly as you paw through these pages.

—*Jim Dratfield*

bagels 'n' dox

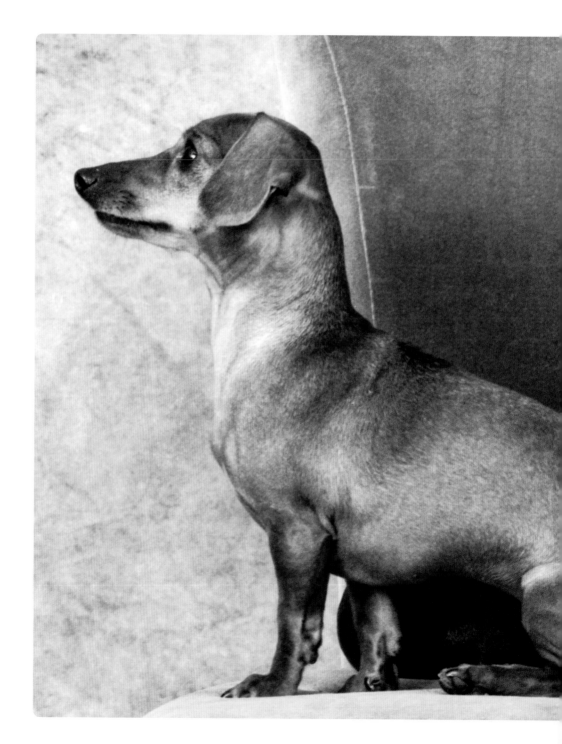

pair-a-dox

pai-a-dox

lunch *dox*

up
on
my
reading

chow

hounds

barking up the wrong tree

barking at the waiter

round
mound
of

WEIGHT
———
HOROSCOPE
AND
WEIGHT
5¢

hound

pooch 'n boots

leashed

angel dog

devil dog

dox

on
the
rocks

inclined to recline

doggie bag

puppy

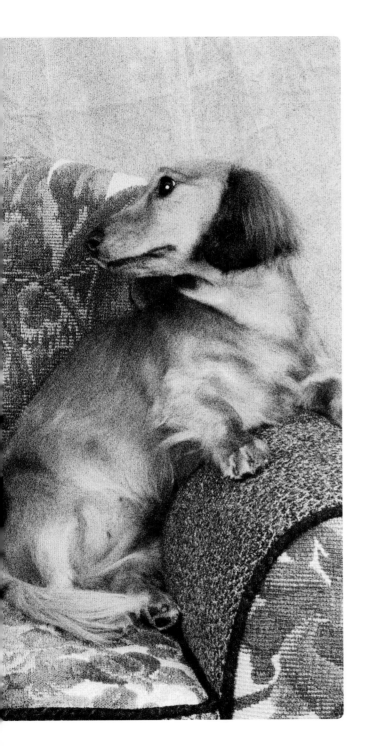

love

scent in the hounds

a snout with

clout

checked

mates

woofer

'n'

tweeter

what's up,

dox?

stoop

doggy

dog

the long ar

tongue

'n cheek

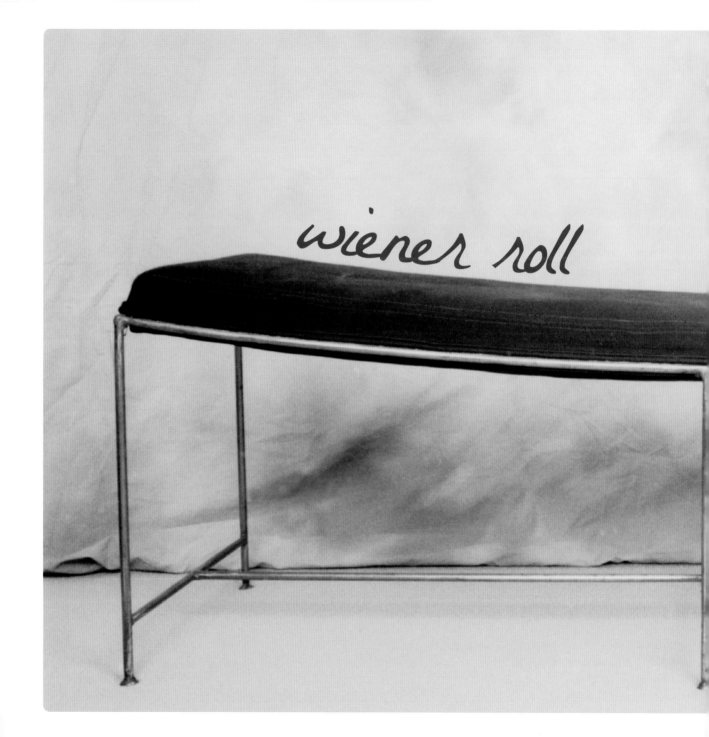

wiener roll

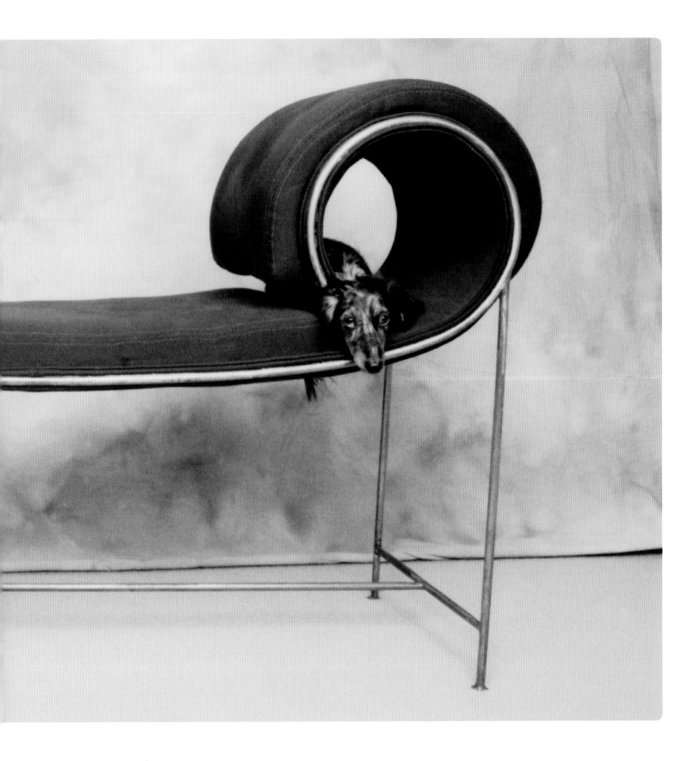

the dog

in art

the dog

out of art

sittin'
on the dox
of the
bay

plaid cad

doggie paddle

you
ain't
nothin'
but a
hound dog

well

stacked

stretch . . . marks

heavy *petting*

ol'
blue eyes

by a hare

sheep dog

dog-eared

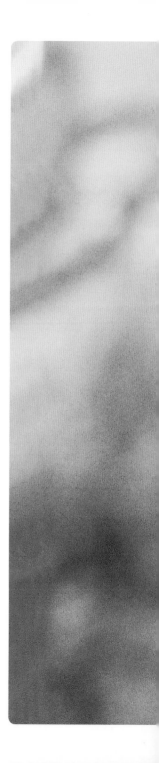

hang dog

dog days *of summer*

dogma

dogpa

the
eyes

have

it

a pup o' tea

ò dogs

got milk . . .

shake

beach

rovers

baby sit

dog sit

dog stand

mail

dox

dog tired

let sleeping dogs *lie*

dog
training

hollywood hound

hounded by *guilt*

pot

head

dox

Zen

kosher hot dog

indoxicated

hip 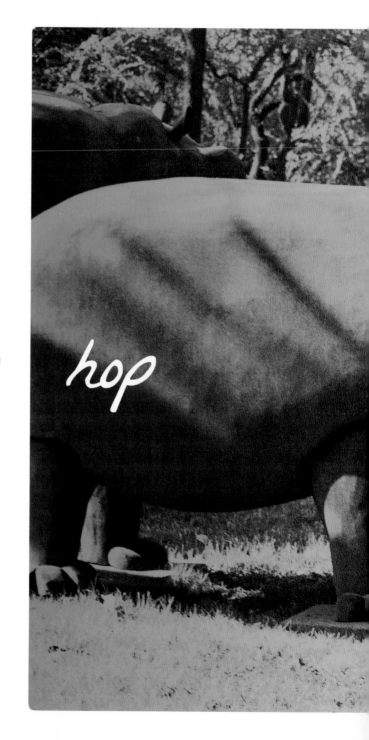 hop

coochie
coochie
poochie

chilly dog

dog

doggone

dox 'n' found

halloweener

cool cat...
i mean...

dog

twinkle *toes*

doxie with moxie

big
game
hunters

links

on the links

top

dog

DACHSHUND CLUB
OF AMERICA INC

doggin' it

for
the
camera

and the wiener is . . .

A SPECIAL THANK YOU TO MY FRIENDS AT LYONS PRESS WHOSE dogged enthusiasm for my work keeps me plugging along. In particular, my editor Holly Rubino who believed in me from the get-go. A nod to you for those lovely seafood power lunches by the bay.

To Inkwell Management, in particular Monika Woods and the wonderful Kimberly Witherspoon, whose belief in my talent has led me to where I am today.

I must offer a special thanks to Adrian and the Dachshund Friendship Club for their help and participation in this project.

To Dikerdachs, for allowing me to include their wonderful dachshunds.

I had a "doggone" good time shooting portions of this book in Memphis and Germantown, Tennessee. Thank you to Amanda Wall for initiating the visit and the warmest affection to Nancy Barrow and all of those wonderful people and pooches involved with the Weenie Run. To Danny Spinosa of www.memphiselvis.com. You are truly the king of Elvis.

To Don and Mary Scholund for loaning their boot to the cause and to Lisa Fortin for being such a gracious Graceland hostess.

To Heather for helping me round up such gems of doxies for the L.A. shoots. To Elaine Seamans, Teri Austin, and the Amanda Foundation, whose love and concern for animals are second to none. I offer a thank you for your help and support. To Tail O' the Pup for their good-natured patience with me while shooting at their historic establishment.

A thank you must go out to all of the humans who were willing to travel near and far to allow me to capture their precious dachshunds on film for this book.

My last thank you goes to all of the dogs on these pages, who humbled me with their character and their unique beauty, a group with an incredible variety of sizes, shapes, coats, temperaments, and personalities. To all of you dachshunds, I offer a final howl of appreciation!

JIM DRATFIELD is the owner of Petography® (www.petography. com) and travels the country to photograph pets with and without their people. He is the author of *The Love of a Lab*, *Pug Shots*, *Underdogs*, and *The Quotable Equine*. Jim grew up in Princeton, New Jersey, and spent more than a decade acting on Broadway and on television. He lives on a farm in upstate New York with his wife Chiara, son Phineas, and their dogs Sawyer and Maeve.